LULLABY OF TEETH

An Anthology of
Southern California Poetry

LULLABY OF TEETH

An Anthology of
Southern California Poetry

MOON
TIDE PRESS

~ 2017~

Lullaby of Teeth: An Anthology of Southern California Poetry
© Copyright 2017 Moon Tide Press

Editor-in-chief
Eric Morago

Associate Editor
Michael Miller

Marketing Specialist
Caitlin Hawekotte

Proofreader
Jim Hoggatt

Front & back cover photos
Boris Ingles

Book design
Michael Wada

Moon Tide logo design
Abraham Gomez

Lullaby of Teeth: An Anthology of Southern California Poetry
is published by Moon Tide Press

Moon Tide Press #166
6745 Washington Ave.
Whittier, CA 90601
www.moontidepress.com

FIRST EDITION

Printed in the United States of America

ISBN # 978-0-9974837-2-7

CONTENTS

Foreword: How We Got Here

FOREWORD: HOW WE GOT HERE

It was 2007 and I was barely a poet. I was just a week into an MFA program with only a year's experience writing the kind of poetry I knew I wanted to share with a larger audience—one that extended far beyond the charmingly odd transients of a certain Friday night open mic spot I frequented, where a man named Easy would sing and play kazoo.

That being said, I was unpublished. So, when Michael Miller, the previous publisher of Moon Tide Press, emailed me around that same time, asking I send him a few poems for an anthology he was putting out, I was stoked. I mean, I had Moon Tide books on my shelf—Mindy Nettifee's *Sleepyhead Assassins* and Ben Trigg's *Kindness from a Dark God*. Whoever was in that collection with me, I knew I'd be in good company.

I wasn't wrong. *Carving in Bone* featured twelve diverse and distinct voices, and I considered myself lucky to be among them. I was (and still am) grateful my first publication was in that anthology, which celebrated poetry and provided opportunity—not only to its poets, but to the readers as well, to discover and enjoy something new.

The next decade saw my relationship with Moon Tide grow; Michael graciously published my first full-length collection after I finished grad school, and I continued to support the Press—both as author and audience. I watched as Moon Tide continued to provide publishing opportunities to deserving poets and was pleased to be a part of its expanding catalogue and family.

In December 2016, Michael approached me and asked if I'd be interested in taking the Press over from him, as he was ready for new adventures, and thought perhaps, I'd be ready for something different, too—to move from poet to publisher. He was right.

I wanted to give back to a community that gave me so much, to present poets (both known and unknown) the chance to have their work seen by wider audiences, and give casual and unsuspecting readers a reason to pick up a book of poetry. I decided an anthology was the perfect project to start off with—to build on Moon Tide's tradition while defining our aesthetic moving forward.

So, I put the call out for submissions, and honestly, didn't quite know what to expect. I worried I was going to be staring at an empty inbox, or worse, have Easy show up on my doorstep with his kazoo. Fortunately for us all, that did not happen. I received so much great work by so many wonderful poets that narrowing it down to the eighteen here was no easy (excuse the pun) task.

Lullaby of Teeth is a collection that offers variety of voice, style, and experience. Here you will find poems about culture, identity, and parenthood, mixed in with alien abductions, jilted fat jeans, and honorary cockroaches. There are names among these poets you may recognize, but hopefully a handful you do not, and (like I was sifting through their submissions) will be discovering for the first time. I hope the tastes presented here encourage you to go out and read more of their work, or attend a poetry reading they are at. I believe a good anthology is a feast of small plates—a 5-star tapas restaurant—that leaves you delightfully full, but not so much that you can't begin to think about your next meal. Or perhaps, enjoy the same order again.

As for the title, you might be wondering, "Why *Lullaby of Teeth*?" When I read this line in Bill Cushing's poem, "Alpha Dreams," it struck the right chord with me—the best poetry is that perfect paring between the hard and soft of this world, the grit and glimmer. These poets do just that, whether in the subject matter they are exploring, or the imagery they use. Collected together, they are song and they are bite.

I couldn't be any prouder to share them with you, and am honored they trusted Moon Tide and myself with their work—they are the poets paving the future of this Press, as we all begin this next chapter together.

Eric Morago
Publisher
Moon Tide Press

Alexis Rhone Fancher

BLACK FLAG

1.   The killer on *Forensic Files* says to his blond captive: *You're about to have a bad day.* I can only imagine. The blindfold. The chokehold. His fingers' dull caress.

2.   Ants crawl up my sleeve and down my dress. I am trying to be humane, picking them off one at a time with a wadded-up Kleenex. But even after I kill, I feel them on my skin.

3.   They are unstoppable—triumphing over ant bait, partying in those tiny poison pyramids, oblivious, probably breeding.

4.   On my way to work I arrive at that stranglehold of freeways—over and underpasses connecting the arteries of the 10 with the 405, where the freeway rises and rims the sky, a momentary blind spot. Or an opening.

5.   On the drive home, I contemplate murder.

6.   I spray the ants with Black Flag. The next day a cricket does a death march across my floor. And then another.

7.   *I have to go pull dandelions*, my friend emails. *I refuse to spray poison on the yard*, he writes. It's like he knows. Now I watch TV all night, so guilty I can't sleep.

8.   The killer on *Forensic Files* waves as the detectives lead him off to prison. I wave back.

CRUEL CHOICES

When my husband's two grown daughters are in town, the three of them go to the movies, or play pool—share dinner every night, stay out late. I haven't seen my stepdaughters since my son's funeral in 2007. When people ask, I say nice things about the girls, as if we had a relationship. When people ask if *I* have children, I change the subject. Or I lie, and say no. Or sometimes I put them on the spot and tell them yes, but he died. They look aghast and want to know what happened. Then I have to tell them about the cancer.

Sometimes, when the older daughter, his favorite, is in town, and she and my husband are out together night after night, I wonder what it would be like if that was me and my boy, if life was fair, and, rather than my husband having two children, and I none, we each had one living child. His choice which one to keep.

Lately when people ask, I want to lie and say yes, my son is a basketball coach. He married a beautiful Iranian model with kind eyes, and they live in London with their twin girls who visit every summer; the same twins his girlfriend aborted with my blessing when my son was eighteen, deemed too young for fatherhood, and everyone said there would be all the time in the world.

UNSOLICITED ADVICE TO A FACEBOOK MOM

Stop plastering the site with photos
of your strapping boy on the cliff
of manhood, pitching a no-hitter,
practicing guitar.

Don't publicize his tuxedoed beauty
posing with his prom date,
or family jaunts to look at colleges for the fall.

Better to shield him from happenstance,
mistaken identity, the evil eye.
Protect him from what you won't imagine:
a drive-by,
a street race,
an overdose,
a dare.

Pass an egg above his body while he's sleeping.
Make the *mano fico* over him with your fist.
Sew small mirrors into his clothes to reflect misfortune.
Tie a red string around his wildness.

When someone gives him a compliment,
spit over your shoulder three times.
Then touch wood.

Stop flaunting your boy's shining face,
his sweetness, how he still
lets you kiss him goodnight.

Listen to me:
like you, I was once besotted.

Don't tempt the gods.

COMPLICIT

1. Mosquitos copulate against my screen door.
   When I flick at them, they float further down screen.
   Still fucking.
   I've known men like that.
   Men who turn disaster into opportunity.
   Call it Kama Sutra.

2. Yesterday my ex calls.
   Another crisis. I can't stop listening.

3. *Every time we see each other, it's like
   we've never been apart,* he says.
   I have no idea what he's talking about.

4. He steps into my personal space
   like a virus.

5. On Spring St., there's a dead rat on the sidewalk
   with stiff paws and a foot-long tail.

6. We decide to give it another try.

7. The mosquito zapper in the bedroom sparks
   and sizzles.

8. That joke about marrying a schizophrenic—
   fuck a different man every night.

9. In the morning, my ex is so up in my face
   he could lick me.

10. The rat is on the sidewalk. Still dead.

Armine Iknadossian

ACCIDENTAL POETRY

Accidental poems are like accidental pregnancies.
They happen to the best of us,
each tiny bastard reminding us we are at the mercy
of Darwin's theory. Three stanzas in
and you wonder if it's worth the trouble.
It might be best to pretend it never happened.
One push of a button, a little blood, and no one's the wiser.
Or you can give it to someone who will tell you why
you should love it just the way it is.

Accidental poems are like accidental overdoses.
Even pre-scripted, they are highly
addictive and dangerous to one's health—
so choose yours with care, and make
the pleasure last. Make it burn like Dickinson
strung out on personification or Hunter S. Thompson
chasing that golden-headed dragon of a sentence
with a hallowed-out pen in front of one nostril
and one ink-stained hand reaching for his Smith and Wesson.

Accidental poems are like accidental suicides.
You pull the trigger every time;
it is not a muscle spasm or an overdose
due to miscalculation. You mean every word.
Even when a poem is a mistake, it is still
a literary form of autoerotic asphyxiation,
every humiliating stanza falling down the page
like an elegant lady dressed to the nines
tumbling head first into mid-town traffic.

ELEPHANT HOUSE

If you look closely you can see them:
one behind the armchair, two hiding under
the dining room table, trunks intertwined.
A newborn stands very still against the back wall
hoping to blend in with the mauve wallpaper
while across the room, his mother tries
to pull the blinds shut with her mouth.
The one in the bathroom is stuck,
her body halfway out the door,
and the one in the kitchen keeps turning the faucet
on and off. The bedroom holds three
big ones, two on the bed,
one by the vanity painting her face.
Outside the roses are being symbolic
with their beauty and many little thorns.
And the birds continue to be the agents
of freedom and peace. Their jobs are easy.
But the elephants have signed up for the worst bit,
and they know it. On rare occasions, they must sit
on a lap, nudge someone in the back of the neck
with their glorious heads. One tried to eat the geraniums
on the windowsill, and another almost tore a chandelier
right out of the ceiling, but nobody noticed.

SEVEN STONES

Again, and again, I weigh my body.
Every Friday morning
I add a stone; take a stone.
I take one foot off the scale and imagine
my hips pain free.
I am suffering for my art, I say.

My breasts grow heavier every year.
One stone for binge eating
after the job interview.
One stone for the ripped armpits
of a favorite blouse.

I feel the fat fibroids
when I lay on my stomach,
a strange non-pregnancy.
A surgeon removed them for me
but did not place them on my lap.
The size of grapefruits, he said.
You lost half your blood, he said.

These non-babies,
once removed, looked like
wads of chewed up bubble gum
rolled into fists
without legs or arms or a face.

My body says good riddance.
Throw the fleshy monsters
into a toxic waste bag.
Toss the nonexistent infants
into a dumpster.

One stone for the man on the bicycle
shot and killed in front of my house.
One stone for Prozac's sacrament
every morning like clockwork.
One stone for my broken left foot,
one for my torn knees and
one more for hereditary heart disease.

Take them and lay them in your gardens.
Put the stones where you can see them.
I don't want them anymore.

PLAYING HOUSE

What genuine promise can you visit
at the altar of your heart?
Even so, will you go back on it
just to suck on tits
the size of hand grenades?
Will you water her plants too?
You gave her a diamond once and got it to fit.
Gave up smoking when the baby was born.
Gave all you had, relatives and all.
Then you got yourself a raise, a son, a small affair.
You stripped the bed, bleached the sheets,
said a few Hail Marys and showed up on time for dinner.
You really wanted it. The life of a man.
But you still want to play in the rye at the edge of the cliff
while someone chases after your young body.
You're going to die anyway.
In 30 years you will buy her a gift,
and she will know what it is before she opens it.

Bill Cushing

ALPHA DREAMS

The wolf bares fangs
even when sleeping.

Legs move
in rapid dream-twitches;
cheeks quiver from tickling
branches that swipe his head.

Leading the hunt,
he chases with others of the pack—
 sweaty fear
 fills his nostrils
 and sanguine expectation
 tingles through his thighs.

Nipping,
then ripping
at the flanks of a deer,
they jump
with him, as one.
Then, the imagined pack
straddles its fallen meal,
dining
without grace.

A lullaby of teeth,
as enamel scrapes against bone,
and the song of sinew,
stretching before tearing free
from the cooling carcass,
fill his night.

FINAL FLIGHT

I slept through those initial collisions,
the twin explosions
as steel and fuel met concrete and girder
for the final collapse
into rock and powder of two towers
meant as monuments
to the grandeur of their century.

I saw it from a safe distance—
not living through events
except for my own recall
or replays of video. I can still note
and retrieve the day, but
the singular image I cannot shed, the one
that refuses to leave my head

is that of people, the 200 left who,
facing the option
of burning alive, knowing at that moment
they were indeed dead,
chose instead, like Icarus,
to spread their arms
in almost-welcome embrace of

the quarter-mile journey back to earth.

CLARENCE

After a lifetime of farming,
tending land and animals,
you retire.

Replacing the smell of dung
with the scent of sawdust,
you take up hammer and chisel
to become a carpenter.
You say, half-joking,
it is the best way
to stay out from underfoot.
You tell that to a reporter from Ames.

He writes that should the Grim Reaper
ever knock on your door,
you'd invite him in for checkers
providing he is neither
a Democrat nor a Baptist;
after serving coffee,
playing a few games,
Death would probably leave,
a new customer.

Like many carpenters
you lose some fingers to your craft,
showing your heart
was in your work—
sacrifice
being more important
than a few manual digits.

And the heart shows
in each finished product:
the wooden bowls
that come from a lightning-struck tree,
the clocks
all set seven minutes too slow,
or the stool
you build your great-grandson—
its seat
heart-shaped,
legs shortened
for his.

FROM CALIFORNIA TO CHICAGO

The rolling surf and mists
of clouds reflect
the sunlight
off the side of our flight
and into the Grand Canyon:
three rock formations snake
through the gigantic gullet,
their peaks like the spine
of an iguana.

The inverted capillaries,
veins, and arteries
of river beds cut through
the landscape,
indentations that seem as if
God had scraped spoons
of ice cream
out of the earth.

The topography transforms
into faces in the terrain,
and we look down on contortions
of grimaces.

Landing, we slide beneath
the bellies of arriving
and departing jets.
*The moving walkway is now
ending; please look down.*
Above, candy-colored
coat hangers of neon
burn and cool the area while
rising up into the concourse
of O'Hare, a plastic and chrome
Grand Central Station
for the new millennium
opens floodgates
for the art of denial,
washes away
all silt of tradition.

Boris Ingles

THE LAST DRUNKEN TRIBE

they say the cockroach

that scaly metallic fellow
w/ egyptian eyes
& rabbit ears

who always seems
to be planning
some grand scheme

will inherit
the earth

but i believe
their uprising
has already begun

last night
while staggering
in my kitchen

i saw one
in my cupboard
staggering just the same

before i could end him
he hissed
pointed
gestured

as if to say
hey
i was here first

i'm still here now
so go ahead
spray & stomp
all you want

i'll be here
long after you
are dust & bone

A MARRIAGE OF EGGS
BEANS & RICE

i sit in this dive
on the westside
of los angeles

order a plate
of huevo estrellado
w/ a side of casamiento

for a moment i'm home
                back home
barefoot in la colonia
de santa tecla

listening to mama's
humming voice
loot riches
from the morning sun

sitting at her table
yolk seeping out slowly
like fire simmering on a hill

i use a warm
rolled flour tortilla
like an archeologist
discovering marrow
in the old country
it's the right amount
of dark
brown
white
yellow

the right amount
of soft
grainy char
on the palate

the scent would linger
in the kitchen
snaking its way
throughout each room
finally
settling
in my belly

WHITE HOUSE

everyday i wake up
peel the layers off
my brown skin
w/ a rusty knife
made in america

then straighten
my flattened nose
so it points upward
into beautiful white clouds
made by beautiful white gods

the stitching
like white jagged neon
stretching across my skin

i go out into the world
                    a chameleon
blending to my surroundings
changing my name
from carlos enrique
to charles henry

i look at my people
mi gente
mi sangre
la vos que perdí
the day after the inauguration

i wish i could break bread
speak my tongue
& wear the brown skin
i've been peeling away

CHATTING IT UP W/ BUKOWSKI

had i met him
i would've asked

what's the secret
for writing meaningful poetry

he'd probably say
kid   don't waste the effort
on making it big

write what you know
always from the heart

don't squander your time
writing & rewriting
poems

just
write
drink
fuck

fuck more
drink often
write the truth

if you can
do all three
at once

be happy w/ the time you have
you never know
when death is rolling near

& don't be one of those idiots
who love showing off
a brand-new poem

Charles Harper Webb

PRAISE THE JACUZZI

Because the vents look like flying saucers, Mojave-sky-blue.
Because the burbling makes you think, "cold mountain stream."

Because stairs ease you in, a silver handrail holds you up as muscles
     melt like butter in a pan.
Because underwater spotlights bathe you in their gleam.

Because the water runs through caverns measureless to man.
Because you think you can't breathe through the thick steam,
     but you do.

Because the roiling witches' brew teaches relaxation during pain.
Because kings, dictators, and world champions soak in the same
     sizzle as you.

Because the foam is headier than beer.
Because its fizz invades your swimsuit; tweaks your rear.

Because no one can see beneath the froth.
Because lips seem sweeter, kissed above the bubbling broth.

Because her body, settling on your lap, feels cool as a spring breeze,
     warm as a womb.
Because the two of you climb out, then incandesce all the dripping way
     back to your room.

WHY HE LOVES VEGAS

Not the *Casino Legends Hall of Fame*, or the *Celebration
Lounge*, where you can linger with a gin fizz and cup
of quarters, lulled by slot machines' cherry-eyed clang.
Not the *Polish Contortionist Twins, The Magic of Rick*

Thomas, or the *World Renowned Folies Bergere*.
As arcade lights flicker like quick mountain streams,
my son's blue Luger blasts scaly aliens into showers
of sparks, blood, body parts, plus for one instant,

a crossed-out skull that means, "I'm dead."
Only his bravery, speed, and marksmanship, he thinks—
Blam! Blam! Blam! Blam!—stop the space-monsters
from breaking down the Nuclear Reactor's *Keep Out!* door

and mutilating Steph, the busty Green Beret.
He doesn't understand, waiting for monster-blood
to spray the darkened halls, that I've dropped no coins
in his machine, so the same scenes replay endlessly.

He caps each kill with a "Yeah, baby," blows a mocking kiss,
and shrills, "I'm not afraid of anything," convinced,
like those who grip the one-armed bandits' knobby fists,
that his fate rests firmly in his own strong hands.

WE KNOW WHAT WE'RE SUPPOSED TO SAY

Would you rather be . . . the baby . . . or the soldier who shot and bayoneted the baby?

—Marie Howe

Up the soldier strides and, casual as a man
kicking dog-dirt off his shoe, blasts
the child between the eyes, bayonets it—

"Dirty [ethnic slur]!"—and marches on.
Wouldn't living with that be worse
than death, the deed metastasizing

in the soldier's brain, squeezing out all
but the need for punishment, the wish to die?
"I'd be the baby," Consciousness replies.

Life's only aim, though, since it blundered
into breath, has been *Keep breathing.*
Consciousness is just a different kind

of teeth which, in excess, bites the bearer,
bringing fear, hesitation, early death.
Consciousness wants *humanity* to stand

for *beauty, goodness, truth.* But cruelty
is human as a Portacan; that's God's truth.
Unless our soldier comes home to citizens

who give him hell for what they more
or less demanded that he do, he'll forget
the baby, or be proud of it. He may laugh,

or scoff, "Oh well . . ." Don't be surprised,
good people, if *you* think, secretly, "The soldier.
Quiet now. I want to watch my show."

LOSING A FISH

for Charlie

Losing a parent: still unknown.
Losing sleep: more time to play.
Losing a limb: you get it back after the game.
Losing a game: cancelled by crying, "No fair!"

Losing innocence: experience beats the didies off of it.
Losing lunch: someone will share.
Losing an "A" for misspelling *tear*: S-word on "A"!
Losing balance: a bruise or scrape, laughter of those left upright.
    Who cares?

Losing a fish, though . . .
The bobber's bounce, turned cruel tease. The current-plugged-into-the-
    spinal-cord, yanked free.
"I got one!" wrenched into "Oh no!"
Ash on the tongue. Formaldehyde. All-souring dark. Rank, curdled
    woe.

Losing homework: Teacher's note lost, coming home.
Losing a baseball: the "careless" lecture; then, soon, a new ball.
Losing Grandma's birthday shirt: no loss at all.
Losing your life: a chance to drop your Blaster, fall on the cool grass,
    and catch your breath.

Losing a fish, though . . .
Death of fun. Fortune's smile turned to a sneer.
Magic you might have lifted, splashing, from the deep—abracadabra!—
    disappeared.
How big? What praise you might have gained? What kind? Perch?
    Tarpon? Halibut? Megalodon? You'll never know.

LeAnne Hunt

NECESSITY IS THE MOTHER OF PAIN

It's the devil's distinction between being in charge and being in control

—Lois McMaster Bujold

There is no failure like motherhood.
I am spitting out the feathers

of all my hopes. A mother bird will draw
the hunter's gun away

from the nest. How do I protect
the chick from the gun it is pointing?

I would throw myself in front of
car or train to shield her, but my daughter

is driving this accident. This house is
shrieking metal and breaking glass.

Every conversation is a police siren,
and every morning a ticking suitcase

she packed for a one-way trip. Yes,
I know I need to set boundaries.

I am the naked emperor of this kingdom,
and she the child pointing out my belly rolls.

I am Marie Antoinette with a saucer of cake,
and my daughter is weaving a basket

to collect my head. Yes, we all need to pay
our dues. I understand the necessity of

death and taxes and a pound of flesh. I eat
my words with a side of liver, gnawed raw.

How do I discipline a hurricane? Or give a forest
fire a bedtime? How do I tether a tectonic

plate shifting away from me? Make her
eat her vegetables and clean her plate?

Tell me about the bird in hand. My skies
are filled with carrion crows.

GOOD GOD

God is good   they say
          Good things happen to good people
Things   happen   to people
          not good   I say
God gives things to good people
          Just pray to Him
No   happenstance is God's position
               The central tendency of statistics
                    is   mean
God is kindness   they say
          to their kind   they mean
If I disagree, then   I
          am mean
My firstborn   I say
Everything has a reason   they tell me
          God has a plan
My firstborn
God is good   they say
No   a piece of defunct satellite falls upon
          someone's head
               but another wins the lottery
          Things happen   by happenstance
Good   things happen to   good   people
People are things   goods   that God
          happens to
Happenstance is God
          meaning to be good
               things happen

SLIPPAGE

In November, the world tilted five degrees
          to the right   in the central landmass
     of one of seven continents.
The ice at the poles slid   a few feet, and
          oceans began spilling off the top,
                    freezing into an arc
backlit by unwatching stars.

Plates   shifted across the globe   inches,
          roads buckled—
                    bent their knees if you will.
          Bridges unfastened   the middle button—
     river seams   loosened in this landmass.

It was a country untying its shoes to walk   away
          from itself
                    until states of being   shifted
          into another state of unbeing
                    until the people, themselves   leaned
                         to the right
                    until some could not remain
                         upright,
     and they   slid   further,
     and others could not stand
               the imbalance and   fell
                    like dominoes
                         toppling
                              right
               until the ones left could not stay
                    and   disappeared.

The birds flew on—the ground calling them
          home—the bees
                    never left the ground at all.

A RADIUM GIRL DEMONSTRATES HOW TO MAKE HER TEETH SHINE

Amelia Maggia purses her lips around the end of a paintbrush
to make a point. She paints the hands of watch faces
as time crumbles. She feels its passing in her bones.

Chernobyl is an animal refuge for the stars. After death,
fur and feathers split to reveal constellations.

Do her bones still glow beneath the dirt, or did they burn
into ash? She paints on a Cheshire grin for the camera,
and the rest of her disappears into the flash.

Lincoln McElwee

RECIPE FOR HEARTACHE

for my Father

He begins with the commingling of leaves, with names like royal and oilseed, Bibb and Batavian, the beauty of these cultivars bending and folding in the hands like memory. Piece by piece, he puts each into his tired, wet palms until his thumbs become green again, his fingers complacent. He collects carrots, radishes and raw onions; old pictures of him smiling in his health; olives and heirlooms; palm hearts and peppers; scrapbooks where no scraps of space are left; the chunk of heart meat's arrhythmic beat. Soon the recipe becomes smudged, condiments end up as instruments, vegetables become best friends' best wishes and he becomes a diet restricted to nurses and hospital gowns. The meat is quartered, the arteries are stuffed, the sanguine, bled. He gathers a few more surgeries, throws in blood clots, pneumonia. I pour another glass of red wine, down another tumbler of scotch – it leaves a harsh taste but this is what the recipe calls for: more hospital beds, more heartache, more headache. When he finally returns home, he finds that the spinach has not yet wilted; the radish hasn't pickled; the carrots will always be fresh. We try to turn the page, to pull the recipe together. But every recipe will be this recipe for heartache. Every step will be a step upon a hospital floor where endless footfalls jolt the heart into action, patience waiting and wading in dressings that are clung to like life. A hunger that loiters, lulls—is never satisfied with letting go.

CRASH LANDING

My downstairs neighbor opens her front door
with a bang,
her Bible study buddies pouring out
like champagne foam,
their laughter striking out like a divining rod
rising to the moon
and then falling flush onto my hushed balcony.

Next to me,
Mars blows smoke rings into the sky
as if he's signaling
the enemy's advance.

He looks at me like I'm a day-old goldfish
he's flushing down the drain
with each successive puff.
As if he's waking from a fever dream,
gaining consciousness.

Music lifts above the rowdiness of the Bible crowd,
while light from a room
where an argument has exhausted each speaker
rises to meet our lowered eyelids.

Above us,
the night sky is a bored child making animals
of scattered clouds,
a hopeless kid forging heroes of stars.

Feeling the strain, Mars stumbles into the condo,
cursing at the coffee table
for stubbing his toe and stealing his water cup.

He's swearing up and down that he has water somewhere,
then forgets it all and heads to bed. He motions
for me to join him
and I want to, but I'm still stuck in the pull
of moonlight.

Mars sighs heatedly, retreats,
closes the door a bit more between us.

Alone and unsure,
I watch a shooting star jet-set across the sky,
wondering where
and when it will all fall down,
at the damage to be done
in yet another foreign town.

Hot rock,
all burning and scalding the touch,
all burning and scalding
to the touch, yet confused at the cooling.

Marvelous, how something
so beautiful can lose its glow and fall
into the familiar.

A lump of cold rock now with nowhere else to go,
elemental and off-course,
incapable of any other landing.

PRODUCTION

He makes a big speech about spending more time with his friends. He wants a solid life, like a real boy. I make a crude joke about Pinocchio and his wooden nose, but he's too immature to take me seriously. Instead, he says at times he feels like an object with me. He needs to *feel* again. So he plays video games with his roommates, racing fake cars around fake tracks in Dublin or Dubai. Tonight, he sends me to bed early and alone, wanting to bond with the boys over multiplayer missions and digital weaponry. In his bedroom, I find a mess of past lives. Leftover power bars, empty energy drinks, multivitamin packets and tennis racket tape; dirty socks, underwear, soiled t-shirts and shoes; sweatpants, condom wrappers, papers with numbers and names, all thrown about because this is how we live when no one's watching. Not the seductive idea of a stranger's smile but the smell of ourselves from the day before. Our honest odor of existence. A one-dimensional picture of his family hangs clumsily above his bed. He says they've never understood him either. But what is to be believed? How do we define love when no one's looking? If I looked for truth among the mess, I'd see that he's merely Love in miniature, a reproduction with a bow and arrow, a lonely boy putting people down to their doom. One by one I'm running out of reasons to love him. I'm running out of space to store such patience. He's a pulse beat and I'm a heart with no rhythm. A curiosity to my novelty. At night, we might touch and even move as one, but when the day comes, we are only ourselves. Dubious, borrowed space.

BELLY UP TAVERN
Solana Beach, CA

The group in line behind me is discussing the incredible difficulties
of growing vegetables on hillsides in Los Angeles,
and how the potheads in Colorado far outnumber their California brethren.
They're convinced that the Midwest is full of roofies and crackheads,
as if Missouri's known history of Hallmark Cards and BBQ has been erased
and replaced by mindfucks and date rape.
Yet they all agree that the air here is beautiful. They describe it as breathing
salt. But the girl from Arizona still can't let go of the smack.
She's pretty certain that crackheads mostly congregate in seedier places
like Las Vegas or Florida. None of them can explain Florida.
It's like an ugly humid penis that tourists put out for, desperate folk
getting horribly done in by bad weather, by alligators, or
Nile crocodiles that crawl around like crabs and sunbathe
in greener pastures like pale white girls in celluloid flicks.
They wax and wane about Montreal and pot, about dust storms, snow
and nicotine, smoking American Spirits, pacing back and forth with such
energy as if the end of the world is about to be born to them right here
inside the Belly Up Tavern. I want to turn to someone and laugh.
I want to feel affinity for the birth of this memory. But I'm alone here
with the night, the sky, these spirits. Inside, the girl seated next to me
finishes her third or fourth beer and assures me she can sense my energy.
She tells me I'm a child of the moon as she rubs my right thigh
while caressing her boyfriend's back. Then she buys me a beer, leans in
and swears I smell like the beach. I wonder if she's hinting at a threesome,
her boyfriend winking warmly right at me. But her lingering hot breath
on my ear soon reveals a sadder story: her boyfriend lives the same life
over and over, like a vampire. He sees the same band in countless cities.
He first saw them with his previous lover, in France, over ten years ago.
That was before his old lover died of a heroin overdose. He never recovered.
Now his life is a cycle of nights and shaded days. The new lover deals
with their dead third wheel, for fear of driving him into his own
untrustworthy hands. The handsy girl passes out eventually from the beer,
her head hitting the bar and her hand slipping off my thigh.
When the music and memories finally let go, her boyfriend opens his eyes,
collects her from off the beer-soaked bar and ferries her away from the concert,
out into moonlight and the salty air, perhaps just as he did before, in France,
in that small college town she told me about, where spirited bodies crashed
a concert like waves. The pressing in, the hunkering down, matter born
and breaking out everywhere in anticipation, listless union.

Linda Delmont

BURYING HERONS

Rigor mortis hasn't set in yet as my son
lifts from his car a SpongeBob beach towel,
reveals a heron he found on PCH,
its wound as fresh and red as a split
pomegranate. *Why didn't you call*
animal control? I ask.

For what, to drive it to the dump?
He grabs a shovel and starts digging
by our back wall. *Don't break a sprinkler*
pipe, I say, my words lost in a fifteen
minute flurry of flying dirt. The holes
in his jeans—over not just the knees

but into half of each calf—
open wider as he positions the body
like a fetus, two feet deep, beak crossing claws.
After smoothing ruffled neck feathers,
he marks the heart with a garnet rose.
An expert at death having already buried

a pet rat, a rabbit, vacation Bible school beliefs,
he gazes at the sky with my father's
blue eyes. This is when I usually deliver
the eulogy, but what can I say about this grey
stranger brought here by a young man
who a few years ago screamed

I hate this place! as he soared
off on his bike into the bleak night,
and despite my fears, reappeared at dawn?
I brush the earth from his shirt, silenced
by the fine line between wings pumping,
wings stilled.

THE COOL SUB

During passing period a student enters class,
cell phone in hand, and says, *Did you hear
about the shooting?* An hour ago at an elementary

school, *some psycho killed some first graders,
teachers too*, she adds as the room fills
and the bell sounds to start third period.

Happened in Connecticut. Where's that?
Others expound on the tragedy as I take roll,
pass out the vocabulary pack left with today's

plans. Halfway through class, no one's on task.
One boy has his head down, asleep. Another sucks
a can of kiwi Arizona tea. Several girls text,

two converse about their love life: *I forgave him
for cheating and he can't forgive me for lying?
Seriously?* The cheerleader who shared the grim

news eats Chili Cheetos with a plastic fork, the boy
behind her chomps a Snickers. In my handbook
of substitute teacher expectations, step one states:

maintain strong discipline. It's eleven days
until Christmas. I think of the presents bought
for the dead, and huddle closer to the Honeywell

heater beside my cushioned seat. The constant
murmur of chatter and laughs seems such a comfort,
I refrain from verbal reprimands, ask instead

if anyone needs help. The girl seated closest
to me replies, *you're way cooler than the sub
we had yesterday. He didn't let us do*

anything. It's Friday at the high school
my own children attended. What parent
will care no work was done? The bell rings

and all exit alive, leaving behind their debris:
empty bags, cans, wrappers scattered haphazardly
like socks and shirts on my son's bedroom floor.

SAVING FRANK

It calms me to watch Frank suck rocks.
Methodically after each feeding, his hinged
mouth grazes every pebble in search

of fallen flakes. A half-foot long, persimmon
orange with a white tail that swishes
as he swims, he's too big for the ten-gallon

tank bought a decade ago when my son won
five feeder fish at the Eastwood Elementary
fair. By the time he graduated high school,

so did the fish, to a pond that turned a murky
green the minute we cleaned it, which wasn't often
enough. They loitered nameless in their own filth,

fed just twice a week yet somehow getting by.
Then the bulbous roots of water hyacinth
choked out the oxygen last August; two fish floated

belly up. In January, a third and fourth disappeared,
mystery solved when my husband spotted a heron
perusing our patio. I searched the house and found

our old aquarium in the shed, not the garage
as I thought, set it beside the kitchen sink,
gave a name to the sole survivor with sheep

eyes that stared as I pondered if he missed
his more ample pool, his friends, or if it's true
that goldfish forget in three seconds.

Last week as I washed dishes, he swam in a panic
from side to side, as if waiting for the p.m. pinch
of TetraFin I thought I'd supplied.

I can't remember if I fed Frank, I said. My husband
replied, *Neither can he. So it's all good.*
Except more often now, I can't recall names

or what I need from the store. I assure myself
that I have the memory of a goldfish, nothing else.
And I feed Frank whenever I feed me.

ABOVE THE MUNDANE

On a gray, dismal day, a vibrant orange Monarch meandered
past my mailbox as I shuffled through bills. *Make a wish,*
my neighbor said walking her dog, *butterflies bring*

good luck. I Googled butterfly host plants, scattered milkweed
seeds amongst the roses as if sowing hope. As the plants grew,
more butterflies came, laid eggs like tiny pearls I collected

for safe-keeping. Eggs became caterpillars devouring leaves
in jars atop our counter. With one finger, I pet them like puppies,
their skin as smooth as the soles of a baby's foot.

It's a control thing, my son said to explain my obsession.
She's trying to control Mother Nature 'cause she can't control us.
It's a mom thing, my daughter said—both home from college

for the weekend. *It's cold outside.*
It's cold inside, my husband replied, our heater stuck at sixty-five,
stuck as I was with a pain in my back, receding gums, gray hairs,

conversations that repeated like the meals on our table.
One by one, the caterpillars transformed into chrysalis to await
their escape. After each butterfly hatched, I said, *Be safe, Sweetie,*

as I let it go. Then on a cold November eve, when the car needed
a timing belt and the dishwasher a new pump,
when between bites of every Tuesday's tacos I said, *Feel*

my forehead; I think I'm getting the flu, my son continued texting,
my husband flirted with the TV, a locust swarm of butterflies
descended from the sky, legs clinging to our screen like pins

on a travel map. As I slipped outside, they spread their wings
like a magic carpet—Monarchs lifting me above my rotting roof,
above my family eating tacos, unaware I'd left my chair.

Notice me! I screamed as antennae brushed my wrinkled cheek,
realizing what they'd brought wasn't luck—but beauty
I didn't have to watch turn to dust.

Luivette Resto

JOHN HUGHES DOES THIS WITH SPOTLIGHTS

No unicorns or rainbows live and frolic in these stanzas.
This will not be a sonnet worthy of Neruda's praise,
nor will there be verbally ironic couplets of
red cockscombs blossoming in rectory gardens.
There will be no reference to the exhilaration
of seeing him walk into the room
where a spotlight, like in a John Hughes movie,
magically appears highlighting the vulnerability of his eyes
and her voice mutes everyone else's—
especially when she says his name,
which never sounded more perfect until that moment,
because it came out of her mouth.
No reference to the synesthetic anticipation
of her scent in the morning,
outlining his jaw with her fingertips,
sighing to each other this is not love.

BREAKFAST CONVERSATION WITH MY OLDEST SON

Another man shot today, Mom.
I don't think I ever want a license.

Driving isn't the problem, mijo.
Driving isn't the problem.

UNRECOGNIZABLE

Invisible hands wrap her face
momentarily erasing the crow's feet and laugh lines
left after only thirty-five years.
Tighter they pull
making her unrecognizable to herself—
the woman she vowed never to be
beaten, cynical, guarded.
When did this happen,
she asks the mirror,
hoping for a response like in fairy tales
read to little girls who believe
in white horses, handsome princes,
poisoned fruit.

Remembering lost lessons from freshmen Bio,
she recites to herself:
the skin is the largest organ.

Tanned flesh,
covered in kisses by Helios,
narrates her story
like the left ring finger
broken during high school gym,
reminding her about the
fragility of the body
and marriage,
or the burn scar on her right knee—
consequence of a drunken college night.

For those privileged to slowly peel
surly graphic t-shirts and superhero socks
from her body, they discover
a fish-shaped birthmark,
poetry-inspired tattoos, stretch marks
left as souvenirs from pregnancies.

The skin is the largest organ:
holder of truth, age, experiences,

gravity's punch line,
porous as it soaks in tears
like sandcastles greeted by the tide.

FRUSTRATED

Why can't sex be
like an Herbal Essence commercial?
Bodies covered in marshmallow white puffy foam,
orgasmic sounds echo off tile
as fingers intertwine,
massaging the scalp
at pressure points of pleasure.

Instead, I turn another page
of the tawdry novel
I scoff at *others* for reading,
savoring last year's Malbec
like a kiss on a hand,
shoulder, or the place on the skin
discovered accidentally one evening.

The protagonist's umpteenth idiotic declaration
prompts me to write about
women who perennially smell like autumn
and eat cheeseburgers with everything on them.

Women who buy shampoo
and batteries.

Michael Cantin

THIS IS A MESSAGE FROM YOUR FAT JEANS

Hey there.
Yes you, leaning over the sink.
You, with your loose little shorts.
You there, crying into the basin like a raincloud
in need of a reservoir.
You know you've got a friend here.
If you really want one.
I've always been here for you.
It's just that you never visit me anymore.
And it's so damn lonely here.
I mean, just look at me,
lurking at the back of your closet.
I don't even have a hanger anymore.
I'm slung over those boots from
way back in college you forgot about.
What do you think that does
for my self-esteem?

But I think you know what I'm implying.
I've never been exactly smooth, have I?
Seduction was never my greatest skill.
I think you get me.
I'm saying that it's cool.
Eat that entire box of Krispy Kreme donuts.
Chow down that Häagen-Dazs.
I'll be here to hold you together.
We can cuddle up in the corner
of that loveseat you used to enjoy,
just like old times.
I've not forgotten you.
I'll always be here.
I think what I'm really trying to say is
I forgive you.

PROVERBS FOR THE SOCIALLY AWKWARD

1. If you must shake hands, do so limply.

2. Commit to one type of soap.

3. Always greet pets first when attending a party.

4. Alone is an appointment.

5. Avoid eye contact with strangers; they may very well be cobras.

6. Water your wallflowers with polite distance.

7. Never drink to forget.

8. An important call will always leave a message.

9. A bird in the hand is still pretty awesome.

10. A conflict avoided is a battle won.

WHEN I ASKED MY MOTHER TO TELL ME
ABOUT MY FATHER

He was a handsome enough man, she said,
from behind a glass of her generic store-brand boxed white wine,
but nothing special.

He was muted starlight filtered through the bottom
of a plastic cup.

He was loyal, like a dog you just couldn't bring
yourself to kick, even after he ate all the
Christmas dinner.

He wasn't perfect. He was likable, but
that likability didn't extend too far beyond public.
By the time he would get home he would have
all the personality of a dented can of shit.
He was a porterhouse to everyone at the BBQ,
but really just burnt cube steak to me.

No, he wasn't exactly a BAD man.
He was mostly gentle when he wanted something.
He was socially square, so at least he was
geometrically balanced.
He was resolute; determined. That is to say
he had a bug so far up his ass you'd have
to shove a whole can of Raid up there to kill it.

He was a mistake giftwrapped in Tiffany Blue.
He was a diamond you had to pass like a kidney stone.
He was a liar and a womanizer and a cheat.

But the cat liked him.

ANOTHER CASTLE

Read between the lines of code
and listen between the chiptunes.
Do you notice the pattern?
These "abductions"
are far too frequent.

Mario, oh Mario,
you think that one day
you will be the one laying the pipe,
but you may as well abandon
your Fire Flower bouquet.

This dungeon is but a stage.
This isn't a quest, Mario,
this is kink—
a princess and her monster
getting off in the role play.

Think about it.

Him:
With leather collar
and all those spikes.

Her:
Flashing her wide empty doe eyes,
talking of peaches and cake,
her palpable lack
of resistance.

Think about it.

You aren't a hero, Mario.
You are the paddle
and the safe word.
A mustache, nothing more.

Michael Mark

REAL TIME

The first days after changing the clocks, either side
of Daylight Savings, I say to myself, *It's not really
3am—it's 2am* or *last week, at this time you'd
already be watching Jeopardy.* Which leads me
to think when I'm eating my mock hamburger,
It's not mock anything, it's tofu and *Your driver's
license says 5'11" but really you're closer to 5'9" and
it isn't because you shrunk—you lied.* Somehow this
back and forth on which time is real pushes my honesty
even more than fear of Hell, and somewhere inside I
hear a voice that sounds like mine say, *You don't really
believe in God—aren't you just hedging your bets?*
But soon those rocky days pass. I settle again into real
real time, flowing with the rhythm as naturally as the sun
coming up makes morning, morning—my patterns syncing
with my regularly scheduled prime time shows, and with
them my belief that the news happens exactly as the papers
report. And, of course, that voice was not mine. I believe
in God, absolutely.

THE COLOR OF MOONLIGHT

On the way into the house
I saw the moonlight
was the yellow of my scarf.

And in my poem the moonlight is silver.

According to science, the color of moonlight,
particularly when the moon appears
full, is bluish.

This is because of the Purkinje effect.
The light is not actually blue,
and it has no inherent silvery quality.

So my poem is wrong.
And actually, so is bluish.

In my daughter's picture, moonlight is
every color in the crayon box.

I tell her it's remarkable and she waltzes off,
repeating, "Re-*mark*-able."

In dreams moonlight is commonly a
white ladder angels climb.

We got home by the grace of the moon's
brightness tonight, when our car lights failed,

23 heart-choked miles riding along
the path from God's flashlight.

Compared to sunlight, moonlight is said to be cold.
I know this is wrong.

Before bed, I read the astronauts didn't think
there was moonlight or if there was, they didn't notice—

though they did report a cow floating,
a flashlight held steady in her two front hooves.

GRAVITY

Even just after we say *Fuck you.*
No, fuck You.
Or when we're not talking for days,
we always kiss before either of us leaves
the house for groceries, to get the dog washed, or
drive to the monastery. The deep all-night-long kisses,
when we're loving each other up
and down, in every direction
the compass can't point, do their job.
But it's the tight-lipped I-Hate-you-right-now-
and-I-hate-You-right-now-too-but-
it-always-passes-sooner-or-later-so-let's-remember-
who-we-are pecks
that hold the whole world together.

FISHERMAN

Because now I have the time,
they've given me the title, *Fisherman.*

They always ask me when
I return, *Did you catch any fish?*
How many? How big? What kind?

Because they call me a fisherman,
they think my success is in catching fish.

I cannot be counted on
to catch fish.

I put the bait on the hook.
I put the line in the water.

Mike Gravagno

IN RESPONSE TO A POETRY READING HELD FOR ACTIVE
SENIOR CITIZENS, WHERE I READ *TWELVE TWELVE
TWELVE* BY AMIEE NEZHUKUMATATHIL

They laughed
when I said I got
my first training bra when
I was twelve
as a gift. Because I'm a man
in my thirties,
and they forgot

I hadn't written
the poem. They wanted to hear
about me getting my first
razor, still giggling.
But I was older. I bought it
myself. And I taught myself

the hard way, with blood
and hydrogen
peroxide for aftershave.
Because growing up
happens alone

sometimes.
I guess art can be
pretty funny.

JULY 2005

When I was 19, at the height of the war, I enlisted. My friends didn't believe I had actually joined the army, so I showed them the signed $400,000 life insurance policy. I shaved off the pink and black Mohawk, took the piercings out of my body, and threw my ripped jeans in the bottom of a drawer.

Once they trusted I was really going, they made me watch *Full Metal Jacket* in preparation for what was to come, and then we sat around divvying up what stuff of mine they would get if I died.

NIGHT ON THE #TOWN (OR ODE TO THE TIME MY FRIENDS
ALL SAID THEY'D MEET ME AND DIDN'T, SO I LIVE-TWEETED
MY EVENING)

I just bought my first bow tie. So yeah, I'm fucking killing it.
Fun game: sit in a dimly lit room, drink most of a 5th of Jack,
then spend the next hour staring at nothing and thinking
about how everything you are is also nothing.

My biggest fear in life is that I'll shave and see how fat my face has
become...
Ok, biggest fear is robots, but a fat face is a close second.

Drinking alone is only a problem if you do it on purpose.

Everybody is acting like an adorable dog *isn't* running around the bar
for just ANYONE TO STEP ON. It's up to me
to show them their error. Smug dog just smiling,
wagging its tail at me, judging me
for not being as happy.

We can't all be like you, dog.

My therapist is a liar, puking is just as cathartic
as talking about your feelings. Sometimes a dog
licking your tears can feel very condescending.

Now strangers are yelling at people for *not* smoking their cigarettes.
The dog and I judge them together, and the dog rules the patio.

No friends necessary. Imma steal this doggy.
Update: I have no clue where that dog is—

worried it never existed.

ORIGIN OF SPECIES

It did not go as expected,
the day the aliens took me,
but they looked as you'd imagine.

Grey.
Routine. There were three
or five of them. Light bent around
their silhouettes, so looking
from the corner of your eye is
where you'd see them most
clearly. But it wasn't
your average abduction.
Not what you've heard. No
butt stuff. They apologized for that.
Said it was one bad seed in the fifties, and

> *better anyway than the vivisections*
> *that came before, wasn't it?*
> *All the blood and viscera*
> *and screaming and dramatics.*
> *At least some people seemed to enjoy*
> *1-Ba D'seid's work.*

I asked why they came for me,
Why my hands bled, why
they came in secret,
why they took some blood—
why they don't come by
as often as they used to.

> *It's a big whole universe*
> *out there between the stars,*
>
> *you have no idea, Mike,*
> *the beauty,*
> *the responsibility,*
> *the crushing vastness*
> *of what's to come.*

I asked if they really built
the pyramids, or Stonehenge
or that mountain and lake
that are on the same part
of both Earth and Mars.
They laughed, or grimaced,
a high-pitched Doppler whine,

> *you all thought we were gods*
> *and we couldn't let you down.*
> *Seemed like the nice thing to do,*
> *build you places*
> *of comfort,*
> *of mystery. To ponder the origins of,*
> *to search beyond the veils*
> *of understanding. Understand?*

No, I said, *that makes no sense at all.*

They shrugged—
maybe apologizing, it's hard to see
the truth in those deep dark eyes,
more purple than black.

> *It's hard to convey the whys,*
> *which we said back then*
> *and you called us wise.*
> *We were just playing*
> *with blocks and shapes,*
> *and it became something more.*

It was only when they dropped me
at my doorstep that I realized
they never said why they chose me.
One by one they grabbed my shoulders
with their four-fingered hands
and hummed something beautiful
that I can't mimic, or describe.

It's all fading,
but when I woke the next morning,
two phrases echoed through the grog:

> *Don't walk home down the highway*
> *when you're drinking.*
> *We'll be back, but*
> *you won't know us.*

I stared down at my hands.
They looked as you'd imagine,

no blood,
just silvery-white lines
etched across my palms.

Nancy Lynée Woo

TESTING THE FOREST'S EDGE WITH A FIXED BLADE

Come back from the dark leave of the forest,
they say. We need you here. Your light.

But how, I ask, wind turbulence and nearly
swinging, can I return when there is no sweetness,

only the mythology of honey? You don't understand,
my light is out, had always flickered. That's why

I'm here, counting all the ways pain makes a person
cruel. I've given up the search for nectar, stubborn,

rotting, sniffing out the best place to rest these ashes.
I may no longer need this body. You don't understand

how the wrinkled fig fits into my palm, how I endure
crushing. The moon, tiny false lash, inverts into

black hole. I see the blood on the cross, understand
how to make a home of pain. It smells of jasmine

as I lower into the cave. It could be nice to stay here,
soaking in mud, savage decay—almost noble. To be eaten

by worms, nearly friendly. They say they want me back,
but there is no way to find me without having entered,

and those who have stayed, have nothing to offer. I must
either crawl up slowly, weakly, severing vines one by one,

or disappear, and I haven't decided yet, whether to convince
myself the fruit was worth the ache. I'm counting backwards

the endless number of ways pain makes a person cruel, bound
to the comfort of the thicket. Clutching tightly to the blade.

THE BROWN TIE

Draped across white wire
frame, tapered silk tail waiting
for brass clip, soft blade sharpest
when worn, both ends
missing patiently
your neck.

It was the first time you left
something of yours here
after I said I liked it and
why don't you keep it on—
remnant of our first wedding
together, fresh toast to new
family still wet on our skin.

It has no life without you,
hanging off my bedpost
in the middle of a room
exploding with bracelets,
earrings, pantyhose, scarves,
dresses for all occasions—outlier
in the center of chaos, we see
each other every day.

You know I have no use
for a tie, except as a reminder
of you.

I use it to imagine
wrapping myself elegantly around you
like a vow the next time you visit,
always welcome and always
too long in between—as if
distance is an accessory
we can forget.

APHRODISIAC IN A SHELL

oysters slip

down throat
reverberating velvet

afternoon anticipation
sweetly spiced to burn

only a little—I'm burning

for a taste, slow
savor of a pearl, you

make me wait, salivating

tender bite on my mind
sipping water to flush

unholy thoughts
out—I know how to enjoy

the feather crawling
slowly up my thigh

just please

don't pull away
meal unfinished

and leave me

dribbling—tell me
this is a game

I will like

and that you know

what you are doing

with that flame

THE FINISHED WORLD

Every log thrown
on was once

huge, underground
& breathing

Some burn cleaner
              than others
still damp from resistant
              dew

       But all decay,
and the flame

sprinkles her lust
for life as far

as the wind dares—
              sitting around a campfire

              the arc of her face
              arrives in licks

mouthing a terrifying wisdom

       you are dying

a tree
thunders in the night

       can you hear it?

Robin Axworthy

LETTER TO A CRABGRASS WORLD

To the way the nodules nestle
and sprout and grab hold,
one to another to another,
metastasize underground,
choke out the soft and green of it—
Bermuda and Kentucky.

To the black crows of it,
rasping caw calling of it,
the ant trails of it, bearing away,
grain by grain, the detritus of it;
to the wicked swans' hiss of it,
and the grace of white cloud castles.

To the iron and rod of it,
the locusts and weeds of it,
the drought and dry of it,
to the din and dung of it,
to the fog and drip of it,
the mud and slide of it,
the bacteria mold,
the death-ridden,
garbage-strewn
miracle of it all.

HOW YOU BECOME WOMAN

One day there are mysterious mounds
lapped by bathwater;
you cup them in your hands
again, and again,
a quiver of dreams.

You find the magazines
your father hides—
you turn the pages,
breath shortening,
small bubbles in your throat.
In the pictures, they have breasts
like plump balloons,
smooth and rosy,
their mons smooth and bare,
as yours were
a month ago.

Now a dark triangle
stained with wired hairs,
fuzzed with animal fur—
underarms too,
odiferous and rank.
You scrape them
clean with blades,
shellac them with Secret,

and boys who used to be just boys
now follow, call at you,
look sideways with scalpel eyes,
push pins of words
into your skin,
which is not your skin now,
but something burning
like disease.
And who stole it,
sold it, wants it?

Not you.

Not knowing who cast the spell
that bewitched you
from you,

knowing only
this shuddering
thread of heat
stringing from knee to thigh,
from lip to breast to toe,

which you cannot amend.

THREADBARE

She says,

> *We do not die in battle,*
> *in some theatrical immolation,*
> *peeled off the pavement, or dug out*
> *of avalanches, or retrieved from falls,*
> *or unpinned from crevices, or lost*
> *in underwater caves, or stopped*
> *by the sudden failing of our hearts.*

She reaches into the basket and picks up a strip.
Green—a t-shirt I wore at Altamont,
kept all these years. She patches it to yellow—
the skirt I wore in fifth grade, braids
it over blue, a bit of baby sheet. And cream—
a piece of kitchen curtain from the old house.

> *I do not expect a quick release,*
> *as when my father stood, fell,*
> *and died that night at midnight,*
> *without a cry.*

Her knobbled fingers move,
left over center, right over center,
yellow, blue, green,
yellow, blue, green.
The braid lengthens.

> *Yes. We fray slowly, thread by thread.*
> *Each footfall takes a bit of wool, a thread,*
> *unnoticed, fades the colors*
> *until there is a hole and then another,*
> *threadbare, like that rug I made*
> *ten years ago that you just threw out.*

She looks down at the basket.

> *I need the black there, and indigo next.*

I pick them out, each a memory, a time.
She weaves them in, left over center,
right over center, left over, right over.

Her fingers pause. She looks out at the tree
they planted when they married, shading the porch.

> *We wear away from days of straightening,*
> *listening, comforting, answering, arranging,*
> *trimming, planting, doing*
> *until our knees and feet and hands and elbows*
> *wear away,*
>
> *until the brain fades and frays*
> *to threadbare.*

TALISMAN

I fly one spring to Denver
to hold my daughter, whose first lover

has left her. While she works,
in fields—once farms—now

open space, bounded by houses,
I walk and search.

It has snowed. A thin bright cover.
The sun brushes the field with sparks.

Like small signposts, prairie dogs
stare and chatter as I pass.

At the side of the path I find a stone,
left behind on this alluvial plain.

It is opaque and speckled like a bird's egg,
quartz and granite—a talisman.

I pick it up. It is rough under my fingers.
I don't know why I wish to hold it in my hand.

High in a bare tree, stark against the bright sky,
a bald eagle watches for prairie dogs.

The stone fills the hollow of my palm as I hold it.
A remnant—hard, ancient, obdurate.

Ron Koertge

THANKS FOR COMING IN

We just want to talk about your excursion on the 27th.
Sunday before last. Isn't that right? You wore that thrift
store sombrero. Move a little closer to the machine, please.
There's nothing to be afraid of. Excursions are allowed.
It isn't as if you tried to escape. We're only looking for
clarification. You and your companion began by
chatting about radioactive waste management. Excellent.
Then you put your hand on her leg. And by "her," we mean
your not-wife, but she of the lavender underthings. Stay seated,
please. We are measuring electric-dermal activity. Nod if
you understand. No, wait. Blink twice. This new machine
is very sensitive. Try to relax. We have only another question
or two. Remember pulling over at the Scenic Viewpoint?
Good. Now before you got into the back seat and
mussed up your uniforms, you read to your not-wife from
a book. None of what was recorded made sense to our data
banks, so we were wondering what exactly were you reading?
Poetry. Really. Well. Would you like some water? We're
going to be here a while.

THE ART OF REVISION

A student hands me a poem, *The best*
thing I've ever written!

I stare at it a long time while he fidgets.

Finally I say, *Poe used to go to a bar*
where a big, green parrot sat in the window.
So he put the parrot in a first draft, but
later he decided to—.

My student interrupts, *Wow! You think*
this is as good as "The Raven"?

I've never told that particular lie before.

Apparently, it needs work.

WHISPERING PINES

After dinner, guests drift into the big room
at El Swanko Rustico. There's a fire, soft
chairs, books.

One of those is Edna St. Vincent Millay's
sonnets. After a glance, everybody reaches
for a real mystery.

I know poetry can be frightening. Who hasn't
blanched at the sight of an open mic, then run
heedlessly into traffic.

But speaking of poetry, in the men's room someone
has scrawled
> *If you're horny meet me by the tree.*
> *I'm tall w/ a black goatee.*

I think Edna would approve: a solid rhyme
with a knack for the vernacular. She liked

sex, too, and slept with both genders. One of her
lovers, the critic and playwright Lloyd Dell,
confided, *She had a mouth like a valentine*.

AL FRESCO ART

Inside the Norton Simon Museum, the pear is on the table
beside the carafe of red wine, the Duchess is smirking
in her blue dress, and downstairs an imperturbable Buddha
watches the bored guard surreptitiously text his girlfriend.

But out here, near the steps, stands *The Burghers of Calais*,
Rodin's sculpture commemorating the brave aldermen who
saved the city when Philip IV of France demanded hostages
and they put their lives on the line.

Visitors usually charge right past it, anxious for more
painterly beauty or just air conditioning, but it is my habit
to pause and wonder if I could get those burghers
with fries.

And since there are only a few casts of this sculpture
in the entire world, doesn't that make those burghers
rare?

I'm a little ashamed of myself making dumb jokes
in the face of such bravery and sacrifice. I love that piece
and would like to take it home where I could brood

daily on what Rodin called "pain, anguish and fatalism."
And then it occurs to me that wishing I could take
the sculpture with me means that I really want these burghers
to go.

Sonia Greenfield

I AM A MONSTER

who has not loved
this body as a girl
in gymnastics I said
you are stupid and clumsy
body and when I
sharpened my hips
with a blade of hunger
to shank my lover
I said *you are dull*
as a butter knife
body and when I invited
body into bed for kink
I gas-lit it and said *you are*
a cum-stained whore you
whore of a body and I have
berated these breasts
for swelling with each
miscarriage and said
what have you done
for me lately body and to
this womb I said
remember that one time
you got it right body
and sometimes I
force-feed body and
sometimes I haze
body and sometimes
I make body cry
and say *you were asking*
for it body and to these
legs crawling with veins
and this convex belly
in which a boy was
built I say *you disgust me*
body and still body

stays so I say *I need
you body but body
you make me so angry
sometimes.*

I WANT A PONY

The medium of poetry isn't language, really; it's... loneliness,
a loneliness that poets... transfer to their readers.

—Dan Chiasson

called Loneliness. I'll corral him
in my front yard, just behind a low,
white fence. Children on the way to school
will bring him carrots and apples, might
stroke his shaggy flank, could stop
to whisper in his ears, which will twitch
to hear such secrets. My Loneliness will tease
the feral cats that slink from yard to yard
looking for new places to shit. My Loneliness
will nicker softly in the night when peacocks
on a neighbor's roof wake us with their
mating cries. My Loneliness will want
to be saddled and ridden through the hills
above the heaving Pacific. My Loneliness
won't mind a heavy load. And when
my Loneliness gets very tired, I'll drive him
to tender and endless grasses where he will
graze, his old gray muzzle mowing
toward the west while I walk back
to my truck wiping snot from my nose
with a sleeve. Then when I get home
everyone will ask where my Loneliness
went. I'll say he was so old. That it
was too hard to see him that way, and my
front yard will stand empty, his trough
dry, his little lawn gone to hay.

HARKENING BACK

We're at a dinner party
with real grown-ups &
the hosts say how much
they love their avocado lady
at the Farmers Market
because she can sell you
the perfect avocado for today
& one good for Tuesday.
I say to my husband this
is what white people talk about
over cheese & olives, unoaked
Chardonnay washing down
all that privilege. Naturally,
the conversation shifts &
the radiologist remembers
when his valley hospital was
one of the few with a unit
for what they used to call "Gay
Related Immune Deficiency"
& *all those mothers*, he says,
*would bring in their sons who
were so young*, he says, & *dying*,
he says. Then like a bell
unrung, I am transported
back to my San Francisco
where these men I knew—
the last of the first wave,
before AZT and cocktails—
would succumb, like my
downstairs neighbor, charming
& volatile, how we would hear
fights with his boyfriend
after too many hours awake
hanging with crystal. Then
he was gone in a weekend.
Anytime I would party
at a birthday for an old queen,
it meant something. It meant

another year. Lo! then science
happened & wards cleared out
& moms got to keep their sons.
Which is to say that distrust
of science sickens me, that some
stupid harkening, a misguided
nostalgia for a retrograde past
would kill the men I love
who love men. No, I don't want
your golly-gee America & I
would be happy to wish you
back into your Wyeth cornfield
& I wish all those moms could
just have their boys back.

IMPERIAL JADE

There is that descent at the end of the 10
where you slip through the McClure Tunnel

and emerge along the Pacific Ocean, the new
highway a necklace of cars strung along

the coast, and you bauble along, side-eyeing
surfers dotting water the color of nephrite.

It's an early swoon if you've had an affair
with L.A. but it becomes as old hat as any

diminished astonishment felt towards
a long-time lover. There it is, just that ocean,

again, with all its pretty stuff. Nephrite is soft
jade, and if you've seen it a million times,

you become jaded, or that's my etymology
anyway. Anyway, anyway, anyway, it's easy

to imagine the boredom of the idly rich,
who glitter on towards Malibu, hoping to

awaken, and you know you're practically
caught in the wind drag of their Bentleys

and their inability to be delighted by anything.
Old hat, just so you know, used to mean

a threadbare vagina, the irony being
it's the well-spring of everything new like

the kid in my back seat who crowned his way
into novelty, every utterance from his mouth

something green, every year forward
a new land to be explored, sight unseen.

Victoria Lynne McCoy

FIRST CATCH

What if I'm good at it?
The hook and gut.

The easy sleep. Can the animal in me kill
the animal I will not eat?

I've managed to keep my palms
clean of god this long. Turned down

every sweet boy with a skeet gun.
If, by name, I've got a finger made

to place a ring on, is another fit to slip
around a trigger, worm down the middle

of a knife's cold spine? Today, I take the fish
in a pair of hands that until now

I recognized as mine, unhook metal
from puncture wound, its fins bristling

in my grip as life struggles out of it.
I watch the thrashing thing fight the bucket

until it is still. I can't tell
if something was lost in me or

uncovered the moment I knew I wouldn't
throw it back, the strange beauty, death

slow-dancing through its little fish organs.
My love applauds me. Slices through the live bait

with a thumbnail, takes my hands in his proudly,
even knowing what they're capable of.

FRAT HOUSE GHAZAL

He just wants to say thank you for the birthday present. He wants
to show you just how grateful he is. He wants

to go where he can hear you better, your voice such a soft little thing.
Locking the bathroom door behind him, he wants

to hear about your weekend plans to drive home to the beach
for maybe a minute until the whiskey's want

wins. The warm mist of his breath on your face,
card and concert tickets still in hand, you can smell his want

as he paws at your waist until he's close enough to taste you.
You don't move because yes, it's true, you want

him to kiss you. And when that isn't thanks enough,
his fingers creep over the lip of your jeans and his want

swells into need. You move his hands back up, slowly, so you don't lose
his tongue. You keep your eyes closed, and follow where your mind wants

to go: the bench above the coast, just before the esplanade slopes
out to the biggest ocean, your safe place in which to want

and to dream, one you've returned to again and again to wade through
all the worst noise inside you. It's a matter of seconds before he wants

to try to thank you again and you're tugging at his determined wrists.
He doesn't have to say it, you know he's a guy who gets what he wants.

When he takes his mouth away, which you've been clinging to
like an oxygen tank, it isn't gratitude he wants

to show you. If you keep your eyes closed, his huffing could be the crash
of the waves, and you know even as you want

to make it back to that bench, you will still be sitting there
in a woman's body, where nothing matters less than what you want.

WHY I BELIEVED, AS A CHILD, EVERYTHING HAPPENED AT 16

after Cecilia Woloch

Because, certainly, nothing big enough had happened yet.
Because that was the age at which I was allowed to drive,
to go to the prom, to date. And from everything I'd seen
in the movies nothing happened before the man arrived
gloriously and gestured to the passenger seat, or stumbled
in blind and without intention so she could win him, this strange
and hairy savior kicking the door in, and how happily, how
dutifully she welcomed him. An empty slot in my kid wallet
for the license, an empty hanger in the closet for the perfect
dress, and all the hollow in me for love and love because
isn't that all there was? At 16 he'd awaken me,
whoever he was, and I'd follow. I'd balance on the blade
of his promises, the way every day after school I'd balance
on the thin brick wall between my parents' driveway
and the neighbor's side yard with its dark mysteries, until
mom called me in to dinner, to sit down with the family,
she and dad at opposite ends of the table because 16
had already happened, and what else was left for them?
This man who would come to me like magic, materialize
on the wall beside me in the soft dusk and I'd practice
my yeses, my dance of eyelash and coy curl of lip. I wanted
to be ready for him when he came. And lord how they came,
they came, impatiently and years too early, but I'd been
practicing, I'd been readying myself for this, I let them
happen to me, because isn't love all there was
and wasn't this love? Because I had to wait for it.
Because hadn't I waited long enough already?

TWENTY-SEVEN

Three weddings down, two to go
before summer's close. Promise yourself,
here and now, you won't cry
in the bathroom at the next one.
What have you become? Silly girl
thinking the world was yours
for the naming. Remember how you envied
the book's loneliest beauty? How she danced
under a streetlight waiting for anyone
to take her away? Dizzy girl
gorging yourself on all that waiting.
Have you forgotten how her story ends?
Put down your fork at this feast of uncertainty.
Put down that fifth champagne glass,
already planning which dress you'll wear
to give the next friend away to another
life that doesn't need you.
The stranger eyeing you by the cheese tray
is not the answer. The man you left
years ago on the other coast
who urges you to marry him
after the bars have closed
is not the answer.
When you warn him not to tempt you,
he laughs at his own joke. Sweet girl,
you are no one's punch line. Remember?
You are the one at the heart
of the dance floor, skirt grown wild
around your hips, brimming
with all that unbridled music.

Zachary Locklin

BRIDE OF FRANKENSTEIN

As a kid, you were always so excited
whenever you found a feather.
You'd pick it up, wave it everywhere,
slice the air with it like a weapon.
You were so fascinated with these
dead pieces of bird.

Once, in kindergarten, we found a whole bird,
a small one, dead in the grass.
We wanted to touch it, pick it up;
we didn't want to play with it
but to recognize its significance,
its deadness.

But the counselor said *No*,
moved us away, told us
that dead birds have diseases and bugs.

Another time in Wales there was
a dead frog, perfectly flattened like paper,
precise like paper, on our path to school.

Sometimes it's as though life,
the process of being alive,
is nothing but the toying with and prodding of
the artifacts of the dead.

I'M A LEGACY, YOU BASTARD

One of my therapists,
I forget which one,
was talking to me about my writing

and I said, *Well, you know—*
(I start every sentence with
"Well, you know . . .")
*—it's a little weird having
a famous writer for a father.*

The therapist gave me a look,
almost like a sympathetically
disappointed look,

like he had expected better from me.

Well, famous to you, he said.

No, I said, (well, you know
really I think I said
"Well, you know, no")
*he's really, like,
an important poet.*

The therapist nodded. *Important
to you.*

NO, I said. *You're not listening
to me. He's like actually famous.
Like—*(I always say this)*—they
love him in Czechoslovakia.*

He just nodded sadly.

I think that was the last time
I went to see that one.

DOESN'T MATTER HAD SEX

At two different poetry readings
in the space of about six days
two different poets
read two different poems
about erotic asphyxiation.
In one, the speaker is choked for the first time
by a zealous girlfriend;
in the other, the speaker is talked into choking;
and the poems climb to a dark vibrant passion
of pleasure, love, relinquished control.
Everyone relinquishes control.

I have written nothing of worth in three years.
One tries of course not to compare oneself
with one's peers, but the comparison
is unavoidable.

Walking from the car a day later,
I whisper to my wife,
The next time we have sex,
could you ask me to choke you?
Or could you, like, choke me?

What? she says.

That seems to be how poems get written,
I say. *It would be nice to have some sex,*
and I could really stand to write another poem.

I can see choking you, she says.

I mean like during sex, I continue.
I don't want to wake up with you throttling me,
chanting, "Stop snoring, stop fucking snoring."

WE SIT ON THE FLOOR

and listen as
the mynah birds
congregate
in the trees.

The sun is lowering
towards the slope
of Kahoʻolawe.

When you woke this morning,
you came to us and announced,

The mynah birds are waking up!

Now, I tell you to listen
as they chatter a cacophony.
When I tell you the mynahs
are going to bed, you reject
that hypothesis:

But it's not bed time!

So I tell you the birds
have to talk to each other first;
they tell each other stories,
they sing each other songs.

And they can play for a while,

you tell me.

They have to play
for a while.

ABOUT THE AUTHORS

Alexis Rhone Fancher is the author of *How I Lost My Virginity to Michael Cohen and other heart stab poems* (2014), *State of Grace: The Joshua Elegies* (2015), and *Enter Here (2017)*. She's published in *Best American Poetry 2016, Rattle, Plume, Nashville Review, Hobart, Diode, Tinderbox Poetry Journal,* and elsewhere. A multiple Pushcart Prize and Best of the Net nominee, Alexis is poetry editor of Cultural Weekly. She lives in Los Angeles. You can find her at alexisrhonefancher.com.

Beirut-born, Southern California-raised **Armine Iknadossian** is the author of *United States of Love & Other Poems* (2016). She has been featured most recently in *The Altadena Poetry Review, Angels Flight Literary West, Entropy and The Rise Up Review.* Her work can also be seen in the *Alabama Literary Review, Arbutus, Pearl, Rhino, Split This Rock* and *The Nervous Breakdown.* Armine has an MFA in Poetry from Antioch and has worked as a teacher, as assistant editor to Arianna Huffington, Robert Scheer and Molly Ivins, and most recently as bookstore manager of Beyond Baroque, a beloved Los Angeles literary institution. Since 2013, Armine has been a Writing Consultant for The Los Angeles Writing Project through CSULA. She was recently chosen by Red Hen Press to be one of their Writers in the Schools. Find out more at armineiknadossian.com.

Bill Cushing lived in various states, the Virgin Islands, and Puerto Rico before moving to California. Returning to college after serving in the Navy and working on commercial ships, he earned an MFA in writing from Vermont's Goddard College. He teaches at East Los Angeles and Mt. San Antonio colleges. He's published in *Aethlon, Brownstone Review, Mayo Review, Newtown Literary, Spectrum* (as one of the "Top Ten Poets of L.A. in 2017), both volumes of the award-winning anthologies *Stories of Music,* and *West Trade Review.* His current project, "Notes and Letters," combines poetry with music and can be found on Facebook and Youtube.

Boris Salvador Ingles was born and raised in Los Angeles, in the small community of Boyle Heights. He enjoys combining poetry and photography as a means for visual and emotional expression, and often mixes humor, vulnerability, and a sense for dark-street-realism into his work. His poems and photography have appeared in *the Coiled Serpent Anthology, Spectrum, Spectrum 2, In-Flight Literary Magazine, Incandescent Mind, Cadence Collective: Year Two Anthology* and *Then & Now: Conversations with Old Friends.*

Charles Harper Webb's latest book, *Brain Camp,* was published in 2015 by the University of Pittsburgh Press, which will publish his next collection, *Sidebend World,* in 2018. *A Million MFAs Are Not Enough,* a collection of essays on contemporary American poetry, was published by Red Hen Press in 2016. Recipient of grants from the Whiting and Guggenheim foundations, Webb teaches Creative Writing at California State University, Long Beach, and is working on a novel.

LeAnne Hunt lives in Southern California with her whirlwind daughter, a demanding cat, and a quiet saint. She is a regular at the Ugly Mug reading in Orange and at the Poetry Lab workshop in Long Beach. She has poems published in *LUMMOX Three, Incandescent Mind, Winter 2017* and *Black Napkin Press.*

Lincoln McElwee holds a Bachelor's and Master's degree in English Literature from California State University, Fullerton. He has also studied literature abroad in both Italy (Dante) and Ireland (Joyce). He loves traveling and wine and books and wine. His influences are broad, though he loves W.H. Auden, Haruki Murakami and Ezra Pound with something akin to religious fervor. He currently works as a freelance writer/editor in Orange County, California. Lincoln hopes to live in space one day, before he sheds his mortal coil. Please contact him ASAP if you can help with space and/or time travel.

Linda Delmont was born and raised in Southern California and lives in Westminster with her husband, two dogs, one cat, and six spoiled hens. She graduated in 2012 with an MFA in poetry from California State University, Long Beach, and currently works as a substitute teacher. Her hobbies include sewing baby quilts for charity and ushering at theater performances for Musical Theater West. Her poems can be found in *The Packinghouse Review, Pearl Magazine, Serving House Journal,* and *Green Prints,* and she is excited to have a new topic to write about soon—her first grandchild.

Luivette Resto, a mother, teacher, poet, and Wonder Woman fanatic, was born in Aguas Buenas, Puerto Rico, but proudly raised in the Bronx. Her two books of poetry, *Unfinished Portrait* and *Ascension,* have been published by Tía Chucha Press. She is a CantoMundo fellow. Some of her latest work can be read in *Entropy Magazine*, *Coiled Serpent*, *Pilgrimage Magazine*, *Queen Mob's Teahouse*, and an Afro-Latino poetry anthology titled *¡Manteca!* (Arte Público Press). Currently, she lives in the Los Angeles area with her three children, who she calls her revolutionaries.

Michael Cantin is a poet and sloth fanatic residing somewhere in the wilds of Orange County, California. He writes fitfully between bouts of madness and periods of lucid concern. His poetry has appeared both online and in print. You can find his work in *The East Jasmine Review*, *Melancholy Hyperbole*, *50 Haiku*, several anthologies, and elsewhere.

Michael Mark is a hospice volunteer and author of two books of stories, *Toba* and *At the Hands of a Thief* (Atheneum). His poetry has appeared or is forthcoming in *Alaska Quarterly Review*, *Bellevue Literary Review*, *Cimarron Review*, *Cutthroat Journal*, *Harpur Palate*, *Paterson Literary Review*, *Pleiades*, *Poet Lore*, *Potomac Review*, *Prelude Magazine*, *Rattle*, *Spillway*, *The Sun*, *Tahoma Literary Review*, *Sugar House Review* and other fine journals. His poetry has been nominated for three Pushcart Prizes and the Best of the Net. Visit michaeljmark.com to know more.

Mike Gravagno is an amateur multi-hyphenate. The US Army veteran is a pop-culture critic, poet, nonfiction writer, copywriter, and podcaster with several long-running shows under his belt. Mike cut his teeth writing for the pop culture site,YourPopFilter.com, where he co-hosts a pop culture panel show, the *Super Hero Hour Hour*, and hosts and arts-based interview show, *Writers' Block*. He cut more teeth obtaining his BA in Creative Nonfiction from Columbia University. He's currently cutting his final teeth pursuing an MFA in Creative Writing at Chapman University, while assisting the interdisciplinary graduate journal, *Anastamos*, as the poetry and multimedia editor.

Nancy Lynée Woo is a PEN Center USA Emerging Voices Fellow and the author of two chapbooks of poetry, *Bearing the Juice of It All* (Finishing Line Press, 2016) and *Rampant* (Sadie Girl Press, 2014). She teaches community poetry workshops in Long Beach, CA, and can also be found online at nancylyneewoo.com.

Robin Steere Axworthy is a 4th generation California native who wandered off for many years before settling down in Southern California in 1983. She has been writing since childhood, but until recently, only in the interstices of marriage, child rearing, teaching, dancing, reading, and historical reenactments, returning to seriously engaging in writing when she earned an MA from CSUF. She has been published in such places as *Cadence Collective, Incandescent Mind*, and *Like a Girl*. She takes joy in the variety of poems and poets in the local poetry community. Her own poetry currently explores loss and recovery.

Ron Koertge, a fixture in the L.A. poetry scene, has been writing and publishing for fifty years. A prolific writer, he is the author of many novels-for-young-adults as well as a very large handful of poetry collections. A better-than-average handicapper of thoroughbred race horses, he can be found near the paddock of Santa Anita Race Track most weekend. His website is as follows: ronkoertge.com. Take a peek.

Sonia Greenfield was born and raised in Peekskill, New York, and her poems, essays, and fiction have appeared widely, including in *2010 Best American Poetry, The Bellevue Literary Review, Cimarron Review, The Massachusetts Review, The Los Angeles Review,* and *Rattle*. Author of poetry chapbook *Circus Gravitas* (2014) and two-time Pushcart Prize nominee, her book, *Boy with a Halo at the Farmer's Market,* won the 2014 Codhill Poetry Prize. She lives with her husband and son in Los Angeles, California, where she edits the *Rise Up Review* and co-directs the Southern California Poetry Festival.

Victoria Lynne McCoy earned an MFA in Poetry from Sarah Lawrence College and a BA in The Power of Words: Creative Expression as a Catalyst for Change from the University of Redlands' Johnston Center for Integrative Studies. Her work has appeared in *Best New Poets, Blackbird, The Collagist, Drunken Boat, PANK, The Paris-American* and *Washington Square Review*, among others. She has served as a poetry editor for the Four Way Review and a Poetry Work Fellow for The Frost Place Conference on Poetry. Victoria currently lives in Long Beach.

Zachary Locklin is the author of *My Beard Supports Nothing: The Facebook Poems* from the Weekly Weird Monthly Press. A graduate of the University of Southern California's Master's of Professional Writing program, he now teaches composition, creative writing, and literature at California State University, Long Beach.

ACKNOWLEDGEMENTS

Moon Tide Press and the poets in this anthology are grateful to the following publications where these poems have previously appeared, sometimes in different form:

ASKEW—"Cruel Choices"
Bank Heavy Press—*"Doesn't Matter Had Sex"*
By & By—"I Want a Pony"
Cadence Collective—"Chatting it up with Bukowski" & "Talisman"
Cultural Weekly—"I Am a Monster"
Literary Mama—"Unsolicited Advice to a Facebook Mom"
Nerve Cowboy—"Thanks for Coming In"
Onion River Review—"Clarence"
Serving House Journal—"The Cool Sub"
Sugared Water—"The Color of Moonlight"
The Lake—"Fisherman"
The Packinghouse Review—"Above the Mundane" & "Saving Frank"
The Paris-American—"First Catch"
The Rusty Toque—"Testing the Forest's Edge with a Fixed Blade"
Weekly Weird Monthly—"I'm a Legacy, You Bastard"

Moon Tide Press would like to also acknowledge all its past authors and thank them for helping shape the Press into what it was, and what it will be in the future. Thank you to our readers who have supported us over the years, and continue to do so. Thank you to new supporters of the Press, as well. Thanks to every poet who submitted to this anthology; your interest in being part of the Moon Tide family is inspiring and we will do everything we can to make Moon Tide Press the best home it can be for its poets. A special thanks to Michael Miller for his guidance, Michael Wada for his beautiful layout and design work, Caitlin Hawekotte for her invaluable help with marketing, Boris Ingles for his stunning photography, José Enrique Medina for his aid in our new website, and Abraham Gomez for his fantastic re-design of the Moon Tide logo.

PATRONS

Moon Tide Press would like to thank the following people for their support in helping publish the finest poetry from the Southern California region. To sign up as a patron, visit www.moontidepress.com or send an email to publisher@moontidepress.com.

Anonymous
Robin Axworthy
Conner Brenner
Bill Cushing
Susan Davis
Peggy Dobreer
Dennis Gowans
Half Off Books
Jim & Vicky Hoggatt
Ray & Christi Lacoste
Zachary & Tammy Locklin
David McIntire
José Enrique Medina
Gail Newmen
Michael Miller & Rachanee Srisavasdi
Terri Niccum
Ronny & Richard Morago
Jennifer Smith
Mariano Zaro

ALSO AVAILABLE FROM MOON TIDE PRESS

Angels in Seven, Michael Miller (2016)
A Likely Story, Robbie Nester (2014)
Embers on the Stairs, Ruth Bavetta (2014)
The Green of Sunset, John Brantingham (2013)
The Savagery of Bone, Timothy Matthew Perez (2013)
The Silence of Doorways, Sharon Venezio (2013)
Cosmos: An Anthology of Southern California Poetry (2012)
Straws and Shadows, Irena Praitis (2012)
In the Lake of Your Bones, Peggy Dobreer (2012)
I was Building Up to Something, Susan Davis (2011)
Hopeless Cases, Michael Kramer (2011)
One World, Gail Newman (2011)
What We Ache For, Eric Morago (2010)
Pop Art: An Anthology of Southern California Poetry (2010)
Now and Then, Lee Mallory (2009)
In the Heaven of Never Before, Carine Topal (2008)
A Wild Region, Kate Buckley (2008)
Carving in Bone: An Anthology of Orange County Poetry (2007)
Kindness from a Dark God, Ben Trigg (2007)
A Thin Strands of Lights, Ricki Mandeville (2006)
Sleepyhead Assassins, Mindy Nettifee (2006)
Tide Pools: An Anthology of Orange County Poetry (2006)
Lost American Nights: Lyrics & Poems, Michael Ubaldini (2006)

www.ingramcontent.com/pod-product-compliance
Lightning Source LLC
Chambersburg PA
CBHW020921090426
42736CB00008B/740